The Promise of Love

Debbie and Jim,

"May you always
walk in sunshine...."

Best Wishes for the
Future,

Marian Ghiardi

The Promise of Love

A Poem for the Heart

By Dean Walley

Illustrated

by Fernando Casini

Hallmark Editions

THE
PROMISE
OF
LOVE

The promise of love
holds a magic for two...

...a bright and a beautiful dream coming true.

The promise of love

means a new life unfolding...

...a sharing, a caring,
a having and holding.

It's a vow
that brings two hearts
together as one...

...together in everything—
sorrows and fun.

It's a promise to master
the fine art of giving...

...an adventure for two
in the joy that is living.

The promise of love
shines with hope
like a star...

...it says, "I'll be there wherever you are."

It's a promise

to follow

"wherever you roam"...

...to share cabin

or castle

and make it a home.

The promise of love
is renewed with each day—
a brand-new beginning's
a sunrise away.

It is looking together
through the world's
    windowpane...

...at the passing of seasons,
at sunshine
    and rain.

Love's a promise that glows
with perpetual youth...

...a cup overflowing
with kindness
and truth.

It's a pathway of happiness down through the years...

...lined with flowers
    of laughter
and dewdrops of tears.

It's a song of delight
and a sonnet of glory..

...a daily unfolding
of love's own sweet story...

...as the plans that you've
    made,
all the things you've
    dreamed of,
all your hopes are fulfilled
by the promise of Love.

Set in Louillow, a typeface in the
Victorian style notable for its
elegance and legibility.
Printed on Hallmark Eggshell
Book paper.
Designed by Claudia Becker.